DREAMHOUSE

DREAMHOUSE
PENNY DRUE BAIRD

FOREWORD BY MARIO BUATTA THE MONACELLI PRESS

To my dear friend Irwin Weiner,
the most talented person I know.

Library of Congress Control Number:
2014956229
ISBN 9781580933711

Design: Jena Sher

The Monacelli Press
236 West 27th Street
New York, New York 10001

Printed in China

ACKNOWLEDGMENTS MANY THANKS

To my interior design support system: Cary and Lisa Kravet, Steven and John Stark, Charles Cohen, Newell Turner, David Ruff, Benny Zale, Luigi Gentile, Cydonia Boonshaft, Elizabeth Sechrest, Walter Kunzel, Taylor Cooper, Anna Garling, Lori Weitzer, and Kristen Ryan and assistants Lina Rolnick, Chrissy Rault, and Erica Ventura.

To my learned and charming editor, Elizabeth White, who has boundless patience and wisdom.

To my indefatigable agent, Karen Gantz, whose taste, ingenuity, and talent know no bounds.

To friends and family: my husband, Freddy, who always has the answer for everything, and our boys Adam, Alex, Benjamin, Philip, Jamie, and Arie, and supportive friends: Barbara, Lisa, Gael, Nina, Emma, Linda, Gilda, Vanessa, Christel, Bonnie, Jacqueline, Gail and Jimmy, Jennifer and Alan, Caryn and Jonathan, Jason, Michelle and Michael, Nina and Andrew, Susan and Jeffrey, Nancy and Marc, Rebecca and Jim, and Nina and Mitch.

And to Margaret Russell and everyone at *Architectural Digest*.

CONTENTS

FOREWORD
MARIO BUATTA

When I first met Penny I was taken by her charm and style. We crossed paths many times as colleagues at *Architectural Digest* events for the AD100 designers—Penny was selected almost at the very beginning in the early 1990s. A bit later on, I was asked to do a "blind" judging for "The Prettiest Painted Room in America" contest and awarded her first place. This room, in a Palm Beach home, represented one of her favorite techniques: covering every surface with painted classic bead board, installed in every direction.

While sourcing for Dessins, her business in New York and Paris, she scours antique shops and artist studios here and abroad, collecting unique pieces that speak to her. Sometimes an entire room is created around one of these finds.

Penny's rooms are inviting and very comfortable, filled with sumptuous upholstery and a mix of patterns and colors that melt together like those in a painting by Bonnard or Vuillard. They can be traditional yet speak in the present or contemporary and clean without ignoring the classic.

Penny's work has an aura of playfulness; she feels that whimsy undercuts the seriousness of life and adds personality to the home. Her extraordinary talent incorporates the romance of Europe's architectural details, furnishings and joie de vivre. She strives to give each client the chance to have a hand in decorating to their taste, whether modern or traditional.

Perhaps one day after I retire I will ask her to bring me up to date, knowing very well that I would be an impossible client!

Who knows? I might not!

Vive La France and Dessins!

INTRODUCTION
PENNY DRUE BAIRD

Interior design, like fashion, should reflect personal taste and style. Just as some are comfortable dressing formally while others are only happy in jeans, some favor traditional design and others seek a contemporary setting. Fantasies, tempered by functional needs, determine how people want to live today. More than an "eclectic approach," which can loosely describe almost all interiors, this approach reflects the client's taste and personality. One might want to replicate the feeling of the grand palace hotels of Paris. Another is looking for the clean sleek feeling of a Jean Nouvel surround.

Homes may seem to be two or five or ten years of individual collecting but they are actually an accumulation and an amalgamation of hundreds of years of design. While there are some regional trends, there is no right and wrong in interior design. Watching the pendulum swing from traditional to modern and back again throughout the twentieth century is fascinating. Beauty is, evidently, in the eyes of the beholder. There is no one correct look. Today, if a home is designed with good taste and reflects interests of the owners, anything goes.

Throughout history there have been very strong dictates in fashion and home decoration. Today, there is the power of whatever the media says is new, or what everyone is doing, but we know that we can still follow our own sensibility. We are surrounded by every type of cuisine, every type of dress, every type of architecture. All this exposure leads to a sophisticated society that makes its own choices. However, the opposite is also true: consumers are still told, "Look, this is what's cool, this is what's in."

We have all seen the unsuccessful attempts at replicating Jean Michel Frank's revolutionary designs and infinite numbers of beige or gray "design hotels.'" Boring, sad. What is stimulating today is taking an idea, a fantasy, an atmosphere and adapting it to personal taste. We can't always go to Milan or Morocco, but we can live as though we do.

We've all been to ice-cold homes and wondered, "They're raising children here?" The trick is creating a real life setting to feel perfectly at home in and being practical at the same time. I've worked with husbands who complain that there is not a single comfortable chair to sit in; wives who have to stand in a corner to put on their make-up. It's time for designers to treat every client as an individual and design for their individual needs.

When I was a young girl, "White House French" was giving way to "hippie contemporary." Socially, the world was shrugging off its traditional behavior and embracing drugs, sex, and rock and roll. Baby boomers turned away from traditional values and décor. Their parents' homes, filled with reproduction "country French" or Louis XVl, were a watered-down version of Jackie Kennedy's White House, much as furnishings of the French monarchs were revered by their courts and copied. "Country French" was ubiquitous. Middle-class homes, suburban or otherwise, were replete with bedroom sets and living-room armoires. But not chez moi.

Unwittingly, my parents set the groundwork for my interior career. I was a spectator when my parents bought their first home and were so sophisticated as to engage a designer. No French provincial for them. In fact, and years later it's even more remarkable, they designed a home that was primarily Spanish. I'm not really certain that this "style" ever existed. Even the color scheme was ambitious—dark terracotta walls, a gold velvet Knole sofa, still in style today, terracotta tiles on the stair risers, tall brass lamps with shades that would make even Rose Vitow weep, wrought-iron and rock crystal chandeliers and so on. While their friends were swathed in Jackie's faux-French, my parents did their own thing in rooms fitting for a decorator show house, And while I wasn't equipped to know it at that time, I can say in retrospect that it was all done in such good taste. So many of their things have stood the test of time, that in my own homes I have pieces of theirs mixed in with mine. Their rooms demonstrate the key theme that, irrespective of trends, good taste, or era, design should be individual.

No one knew this as well as Barbara D'Arcy, the brilliant and prolific design director of Bloomingdale's from 1953 on for decades. The world may have been changing so fast that one couldn't keep up with changes in social behaviors, women's rights, technology and retail methods but D'Arcy didn't put forward "a one size fits all" look at Bloomingdale's. The home furnishing floor was a veritable designer show house in and of itself. The vignettes all around the floor were like Christmas windows, loaded with design elements to discuss and evaluate. Each vignette was its own theme and I doubt that anyone who liked the French Normandy farmhouse would like the gray flannel and lucite living room pit! Except me, of course.

So as I developed an interior design practice, incorporating study of classical design, architecture, European design, and psychology, there wasn't even a question that design could be universal, i.e. that I could select one single look for others or even for myself.

Every one is entitled to a DREAMHOUSE!

PALM BEACH
PIED À TERRE

Above: A Hermès scarf, painted on the powder room ceiling, was the inspiration for the color accent in the apartment.

Opposite: In the dining area, an elegant Art Nouveau light fixture hangs above an Art Deco dining table and chairs with contemporary fitted slipcovers.

A weekend escape sounds so relaxing, and what could be more fun than a getaway home near the sun and ocean? With children grown but professional life still centered on the gray days of winter, a pied-à-terre in Palm Beach was the next step for a New York couple.

Over the years I had designed rooms for this couple in their suburban Tudor house, and we had developed a strong relationship. The Palm Beach flat was a departure in every way from their family home, something cool and modern where they could escape on almost all winter weekends.

The building itself is a modern high rise on the Atlantic ocean, and terraces and lovely views surround the apartments. The architecture was bland and uninteresting, but since the interior was to be contemporary, that did not pose a problem. Although we had not intended to do too much construction, it was necessary to redo the bathrooms, kitchen, and a bit more.

The backdrop of the living room is a contemporary, clean palette. The sofas are white and spare, the tables a mix of Old World and modern. There's a hint of Napoleonic influence to the feel of the room, while contemporary art gives a sophisticated and chic look.

The dining area was separated from the living area by a lower ceiling height and an unsightly column. Rather than fight it, we cordoned it off even more. I designed a low wall around the dining area and added thin square columns. This created a special dining area with its own charm and distinction—further enhanced by painting the walls a slightly different color.

In the master bedroom, we decided a softer look, with pale blues and creams and taffeta draperies, but still kepy it hip with vintage, midcentury furniture and draperies surrounding the bed. The feeling is crisp, clean, welcoming, and very "vacation." With this apartment we created a feeling of a super hotel suite, and way before there was a trend called "design hotels."

Left: In the living room, the eclectic mix of furnishings, with bronze guéridons flanking a contemporary sofa, a glass-topped coffee table dotted with antique collectibles, and contemporary art, reads as completely "today." The pen and ink drawings are by Bob Justin.

Below: Color is introduced through the art collection rather than the finishes or fabrics, leaving a cool palette that could be enhanced by any color direction in the future.

Opposite: The powder room with its "Hermès canopy."

Below and opposite: The simple "bones" of the master bedroom are enhanced by textured wallpaper imitating coffered walls. Luxurious taffetas encase the bed.

Below and opposite: The guest room is crisp and welcoming. The walls are upholstered in camel stitched fabric, which adds a luxurious touch.

COUNTRY
CALM

Above: A midcentury lighting fixture, purchased at the Marché aux Puces, adds both whimsy and focus to the vaulted ceiling over the dining area in the kitchen.

Opposite: The cool palette of white and gray highlighted with blues creates a feeling of serenity in the dining room.

When young couples move from the city to the country, they imagine they will have all the space they need, but such is not always the case. Sometimes the imagined space is quickly overrun, especially with a family of five. And three little children also create quite a commotion, so the question is how to create a serene atmosphere in a busy country home.

The house is a two-story Colonial in need of a face-lift, with the kitchen demanding immediate attention. We created a large kitchen, breakfast room, mudroom area, office, laundry and powder room. To give the mudroom some pizzazz, we clad the entire addition in beadboard, running it in all different directions and painting it white with the trim in charcoal gray. The effect is charming and peaceful. In the breakfast room we clad the vaulted ceiling with wainscoting as well, painting it turquoise blue, the accent color for the kitchen.

As we worked on the other rooms, we considered the lifestyle of the family as well as their personal aesthetic. The look we were after was modern yet fitting in a country setting—young, fresh, chic yet peaceful, and above all practical.

The entrance foyer sets the stage. It has an open feeling, and the selection of furniture is light and inviting. The sweeping staircase with its woven carpeting adds to this expansive feeling. The plan is organized so that all rooms open to the center hall and to one another. The color scheme—browns, cocoas, and pale blue accents—adds to that feeling of calm and peacefulness.

In reviewing the plan, we found that the butler's pantry seemed unnecessary. We considered combining the space with the dining room, but that would have presented its own problems, including an off-center bay window. Instead we designed a sophisticated bar room, employing luxurious materials such as mahogany, lava stone, and beautiful églomisé from Miriam Ellner. We wanted a functional bar, but we wanted to eliminate any kitchen-y look so we hid

Above: The traditional architecture of the house includes a gabled entrance porch and dormers above.

Opposite: The bay window in the library is a cozy perch for gazing out on a snowy day.

the sink behind the cabinet doors. The bar was designed with sliding doors that open entirely to the dining room. Guests would be shown into a dark and snazzy bar for cocktails and then, voilà! the doors would open and guests would view the dining room and be escorted to their next course.

The dining room was furnished almost entirely with pieces from the Marché aux Puces in Paris. An Art Deco period dining table and sideboard, a midcentury modern chandelier, and accessories combine to create an elegant setting for dinner parties. We wanted to have some additional seating, but extra chairs seemed mundane. That dilemma was solved by fabricating four chair-height poufs in different colors that can be pulled up to the dining table at the last minute.

Below and opposite: The entrance foyer's mission: elegance and practicality. The vintage console and mirror from the Marché aux Puces are handsome yet indestructible. Whimsical pillows from Holland & Sherry add a luxurious touch.

Opposite and below: The dining room is serene and sumptuous. The vintage Art Deco dining table and buffet provide classic backdrops for Christofle china and crystal, J. Robert Scott glass jugs, and lithographs by Jean Dubuffet. Tufted stools in four shades of gray create a window seat and additional seating for the dining table.

Opposite: Large double doors open from the butler's pantry to the dining room. The mahogany cabinets house a working bar including an interior sink.

Below: A geometric pattern of marble tiles is an elegant and practical solution for the flooring in the butler's pantry.

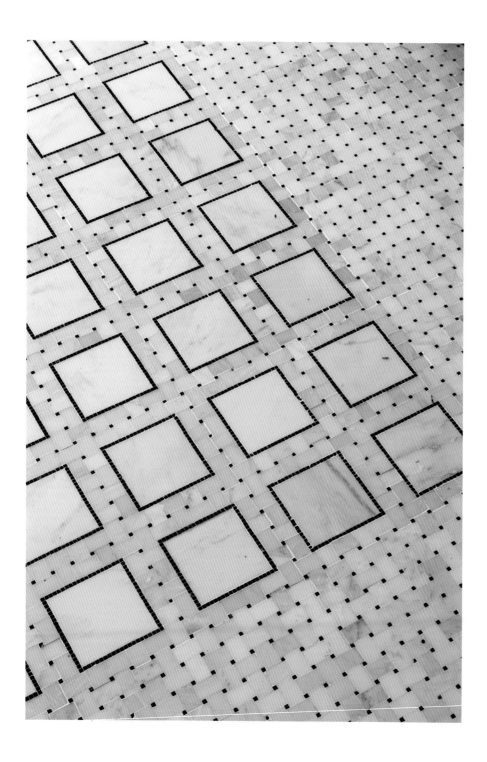

Opposite and below: The simple feeling of the kitchen belies the numerous details including iridescent glass tiles above the cabinet counter, the custom marble grill cover, and imported nickle hardware.

Opposite: Beadboard is a very useful architectural element in making a dull space fabulous; this mudroom is almost too elegant for its function.

Below left: The kitchen powder room is embellished with a chunky, handsome marble sink.

Below right: The turquoise and blue scheme in the kitchen is echoed in the china cupboard.

Right: Too often a desk area is carved out of the kitchen, but here the clients have the luxury of a spacious home office executed in a black-and-white scheme seen in the pony rug, the Missoni striped sofa, the geometric pattern on the shades, and the unusual cantilevered lampshade chandelier.

CITY CHIC

Above: Gracie wallpaper adds timeless glamour to every setting.

Opposite: In the entrance hall, handsome pearlized wall paint is complemented by sterling silver reveals and hardware by Nanz.

How to design an apartment for the chicest person I know? That's easy: do it together. The challenge began with the space. Once a New York City "Classic 8," the apartment had been gutted to approximate a loft space. It would have been possible, of course, to go back to the original layout, but that would have produced a cramped and outmoded design that would not serve a contemporary lifestyle. Young client, young and growing family, young architect: a perfect storm to take a prewar apartment with no walls and create a workable family home, on a quest for urban chic.

Good design relationships can evolve into a camaraderie between clients and designer. In this case, the project began that way since the owner was a veteran of design collaborations with me and had been a friend from the start. Nevertheless, the envelope would be pushed as her tastes, vision, and sense of self had evolved over the years. This apartment, modern yet studded with antiques and vintage pieces, is a far cry from the Parisian maisonette I worked on some fifteen years earlier. Those days were all about provincial French and charm. Today's charm is of a different sort, one that is sophisticated and handsome.

What creates the ambiance here is the unmistakable personality of the clients coming through. Collections, while subtle, are everywhere—jars filled with colored sugars collected in Europe, tea canisters in an array of pastels from Ladurée and others, vintage art books, and antique silver. This collector is personal and private about her favorite things.

The juxtaposition of all these objects and the modern architecture and modern upholstered pieces, as well as the modern art collection, creates a unique space. Take, for example, the collection of vintage ironware and horn boxes on the minimalist mantel or the groups of shagreen boxes on the Giacometti cocktail table and mirrored flea market find. The vintage and antique furniture selections illustrate the client's appreciation of the beauty, quality, and

workmanship of old things. When these rooms are scrutinized, it is clear that there is an abundance of patinated pieces that somehow add up to a modern look.

Perhaps the greatest challenge was the dining room, an unattractive space with one angled wall. Working with Nava Architects, we made a coherent space by angling all the corners. In detailing and furnishing, the room elegantly integrates old and new. The moldings I chose are clearly contemporary but they surround Gracie silver tea paper in a centuries-old design. The floor is reclaimed French oak parquet—a gesture to green design (a concern of the clients) as well as beauty—but I stained it a light gray, a completely modern departure for a vintage floor. The light fixtures are 1930s French, in bronze, a finish that most modernists shy away from, and the dining chairs are vintage 1930s while the table is contemporary. The table is elegant in its simplicity and, although quintessentially modern, it is a perfect mate for the clean lines of the early-twentieth-century chairs.

Similarly, the master bedroom combines traditional and contemporary pieces and finishes. The wall paint, for example, is a modern finish that exudes sheen and texture, and yes, is an age-old technique. The headboard is an exquisite velvet embroidery, fabricated into a simple profile. The nightstands are contemporary, while the chandelier is a nineteenth-century crystal *chef d'oeuvre* that could be equally at home in a chateau. A sumptuous mélange of luxurious textures, mixing old and new, makes this master bedroom truly eclectic.

Below: The sensuous effect of the library is achieved through a combination of high gloss paint on the walls, tactile velvets and satins, and a rich palette of plum and shades of gray.

Opposite: In the kitchen the gray and white veining of the marble is echoed in the window shade.

Right: The historic patterns of Gracie wallpaper are unexpected in a modern setting, but the luminous silver ground creates a luxurious atmosphere in the dining room. The ceiling lights and bronze Art Deco chandeliers are from Carlos de la Puente. The table was made by Mark Luedeman to marry with vintage chairs.

Left: The living room is a true marriage of contemporary architecture and vintage and modern furnishings. Polished plaster walls reflect light throughout the day.

Below: The handsome fireplace was designed by architect David Ruff. To the right is a Sugimoto photograph.

Opposite: In the master bedroom strié-painted walls add texture. A vintage chandelier from Sylvain Lévy-Alban, Paris, provides glamour and drama.

PALM DESERT DREAMING

Above and opposite: Tuscan terracotta roofing tiles add charm and authenticity to the entrance.

Golf is the main event at the Madison Club, an exclusive enclave in Palm Desert. It is a magical place, with luxuriant foliage embracing thirty or so vacation homes. The club house itself has a sumptuous setting, so well done that it seems to have been there always.

Designed by BAR Architects, the houses at the Madison Club are a nod to the architecture of Tuscany, built in stone and stucco. The Mediterranean style blends well with the desert landscape, creating an envelope for a casual, warm, and elegant interior. This residence, which belongs to a favorite client, is used as a weekend getaway, a place to gather with friends after a day of golf with an outdoor fire and a great glass of Bordeaux.

Our interior design marries the architecture with the client's preference for classic traditional design. He wanted warm and welcoming spaces, casual enough and practical enough to withstand a crowd of guests. One of the main considerations was color. Often in Mediterranean houses there are so many natural elements—stone, wood, and other neutral finishes—that the interiors can look bland. It was also important to distinguish this residence from others I had completed for the client. In this case, I did it with color, using a French blue taken from an antique rug as the accent color for the main entertaining rooms and master suite. But it also is an unexpected color in Tuscany, both historically and today. Blues (and whites) are often found in the south of France, but these cool tones are unusual in Tuscany, where golds, reds, and other earthy colors predominate. The blue helped anchor the rooms and provide a depth and richness that can be missing with a neutral scheme. Each of the guest rooms has its own color palette—one is orange, another oxblood and oyster, and the last blue and gold.

Furnishings were selected for comfort as well as style. Here we looked for texture and interest. Many of the upholstered pieces are trimmed with wood, or wrought iron, and fabrics are

Opposite and above: The dining room opens onto the patio and the pool beyond.

woven natural fibers, with chenilles, cotton velvets and linens in abundance. Apart from the heirloom rug in the living room, the rugs are natural woven sisals and tweedy wools.

The owner is a collector, and the furnishings and the objects relate well to each other. Neutral wall colors provide a backdrop for the large collection of nineteenth-century Native American art. A collection of bronze sculptures, many with western motifs, adds a masculine element to the guest rooms and master suite.

As with many interiors, the whole is much more than the individual parts. Here, we created not a living space but a lifestyle, one that I can say from experience is very hard to leave.

Left: Desert homes can look monochromatic, dull, and brown. Here we worked from a heirloom rug to infuse the room with a blue accent.

Opposite and below: Guest rooms welcome family
and friends with warm colors.

Opposite: The kitchen is a handsome combination of creamy tile and rich woods.

Below, left: The main powder room has a desert look with onyx accents and hand-painted terracotta wallpaper.

Below, right: The pool surround is accented with vivid blue tiles.

AMERICAN COUNTRY

Above and opposite: The banister, designed by Irwin Weiner, incorporates antique wrought-iron farm tools.

In the heart of Bucks County, winding roads, lush greenery, stables, barns, and farmhouses create a picturesque atmosphere far from the bustle of the city. As a Francophile and a lover of the French countryside, Tuscany and the Cotswolds, I truly appreciate this wonderful rural ambiance.

Nestled along one of these winding roads, on the edge of Lake Nockamixon, is an imposing barn that has risen from its derelict former self to take its place as a bucolic gem. This barn, which sits on a property belonging to longstanding clients, now serves as the guesthouse and entertainment center for their farmhouse. At first, the clients considered it just a very old and decrepit barn, but eventually it became their dream to restore it to its former glory. A talented colleague had the ingenious idea of removing the interior wood lining of the barn and installing it on the exterior to help to keep the structure authentic. Inside we created a single space with specific areas for gathering, TV viewing, playing pool, reading and writing, and dining. An open kitchen gives on to a fourteen-foot-long dining table, which also was made from barn siding. The ends of the space are crowned with loft-like areas, one housing two bedrooms and a bathroom, and the other a meditation and yoga space. Architecturally, the dilemma was how to access these two second-story areas on opposite sides of the barn. This was ingeniously solved with a dramatic center staircase of wood planks without risers and another hidden behind the fireplace so it completely disappears.

Many of the features of this barn are whimsical. The powder room incorporates early American elements—a copper bowl, a water pump, a slab of wood. The potting room features a wooden table purchased in the Marché aux Puces in Paris. We removed the plateau top and arranged for it to slide, revealing a copper planting sink within. The floor of the entrance is made of cross-grained blocks of wood laid as cobblestones and varnished. A bannister created from old barn tools by a local ironmonger (my colleague's brainchild) lines the steps up to the main living space.

Above: To navigate the barn space, two staircases were added, one exposed and one concealed.

Opposite: The redwood exterior of the barn was its original interior.

All the kitchen cabinets are created from old crates and barn siding, with some of the original wording still evident. The fireplace is a composite piece that combines a French farmhouse limestone mantel purchased in Paris and new limestone added in order to create an overmantel befitting a barn. An earthy palette of cocoas and coppers pervades the space, seen in fabrics—velvets, wools, and rustic needlework. There are many collections throughout, including antique majolica, cowbells, tin coffee makers, and coffee grinders, which add to the barn's charm. One of the most interesting aspects of this barn is that in a just few rooms, there are so very many things to look at. It is a treat to the eyes and a source of constant pleasure for the owners.

Below: Seating in the main living space is grouped around the fireplace. Whimsical accessories add warmth to the decor.

Opposite: Vintage carriage lights from the Marché aux Puces illuminate the dining space.

Opposite: The loft above the living room seating group accommodates yoga and TV space.

Below: The kitchen cabinets were made from wooden barn siding.

Right: Stairs from the entrance and planting room to the main floor.

Below: Bedrooms in the sleeping loft are separated by a quaint bathroom.

Opposite: Living area and billiard table seen from the sleeping loft.

PARK AVENUE MODERN

Above: The living room carpet is a two-level or high/low pattern with two types of stitchery.

Opposite: A pair of 1920s French consoles with mirrors above flank the opening between the entrance hall and the living room.

We may think of white as a single color, but I can assure you it is not. There's linen white, dove white, china white, and those are only a few of the names I've memorized. There is also just white. This is the white we think of as paper, as snow, as toothpaste. It is the whitest of whites. And it is the favorite color of a client who not only loves the color but also saw it as a background for the look and feel she and her husband wanted to create for their family apartment. This was not really a challenge since white is a favorite of mine as well. It became interesting when I had to find everything we wanted in the exact shade: not ecru, not nacrè, not creamy, just white.

Color is vital in creating the mood and feeling of a room's decor. Certain periods of design are defined by their colors. In a modern setting, the background is often white or a pale neutral, with stronger colors, such as shades of gray or blue, adding the accents, as they do in this apartment. Although white played a major role, practicality was essential for this family with young children. I used dark grays as the basis for all seating—thick, plush materials that added luxury and refinement to the overall look. In plan the space radiates from the entrance foyer, or center, outwards, so the flow of color and consistency from room to room is integral to the look of this apartment. The accent colors were repeated throughout but in varying combinations.

The plan and detailing of this prewar apartment did not work for contemporary family life style and modern idiom. To accommodate the young family, two rooms were combined to create a large family room/den that would serve as a TV room, computer center, and dining area. The library was enlarged, and a more gracious and spacious entry was created.

To distinguish a conventional prewar living room, we installed a multi-arched, undulating ceiling. On its own in the empty white room, the ceiling was astonishing. To balance it, we added a reverberating row of vertical raised panels below a high chair rail. Both of these

elements come from classic Roman and Greek design, but they are incorporated in a completely modern way. Angular, tailored plaster moldings were installed throughout the apartment, defining specific areas and adding elegant visual interest. Moving walls made the rooms more gracious, but in the process varying ceiling heights, cross beams, and risers were revealed. With creative architectural strategies, a good eye, and a bit of handwringing, we were able to smooth out those irregularities.

The best clients a designer can have are those with wonderful taste who know what they like. I was very lucky to work with this couple who struck a perfect balance between presenting their own ideas and embracing new ones—the cornerstone of a good team.

Opposite: The family den is all about comfort. The built-in cabinetry is painted faux bois in gray, and the motif on the doors was inspired by a Parisian front door.

Right: I designed this front door based on geometric elements seen in the raised panels and repeated in the plaster molding above and in the bronze inlay above the baseboard.

Left: The undulating ceiling is the pièce de résistance of the living room, which features a mix of midcentury and contemporary pieces.

Below: A pair of wood and shagreen end tables anchors the sofa.

Left and opposite: Classic Haussmannian wainscoting was added in the living room, complementing a pair of Art Deco cabinets and a game table from the Marché Biron in Paris. The chairs are contemporary, designed by Philippe Hurel.

Below and opposite: The library is trimmed with panel moldings enhanced by color variations including silver leaf. The unusual lampshade chandelier was designed for the apartment by Denis Collura.

Opposite: The dining table, topped with back-painted glass, was designed by Philippe Hurel.

Below: The table setting includes pieces by Hermès, Christôfle, and St. Louis.

Opposite: The kitchen is classic, with white recessed panels with a high gloss finish.

Left: A Damien Hirst lithograph enhances the turquoise banquette area.

Below and opposite: Hot pink, black, and gray enliven the daughters' rooms. Vintage pieces and custom lighting complete the fun, yet practical, spaces.

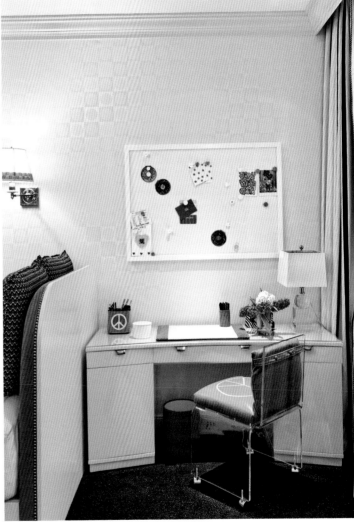

SUBURBAN SAVVY

Above: A garland of pebbles inset into the garden path.

Opposite: The stencil design, painted when the owners first bought the house, has stood the test of time.

When I met the owners of this lovely Tudor-style house, the wife was expecting her second child. Now that child is college bound. Little did we all know when we began that our relationship would generate a portfolio of four projects together that would grace the pages of *Architectural Digest* and lead to a life-long friendship.

This house, our first project together, was a coming-of-age project, truly the culmination of all the couple's hopes and dreams, the home where they would raise their children and the backdrop for their day-to-day life. Over time, their children grew, and their interests evolved. Recently, they called to say that they were ready for a change. They loved their furnishings, and they loved collecting them, but as their tastes and lifestyle matured, they moved from striving to be so grown up, as many young couples do, to trying to feel younger.

This project was more a pleasure than a challenge. The idea was to change many of the backgrounds and create a new setting for their elegant pieces. This often happens over a lifetime of living in one place. While designers like to say that the lifespan of furnishings is ten years, our furnishings actually last much longer. As a result, we tend to focus elsewhere—on second homes or travel or art collections—and neglect the freshening of our home base.

Here, we did little that was structural on the main floor, focusing more on backgrounds, reupholstery, and rearranging. We grouped accessories differently, highlighting those that were lighter and fresher. For example, sculptural or architectural pieces, such as tazzas, stayed, and everything that was "Louis" took its place in a cupboard. Where necessary, we acquired key pieces—tables with clean lines and a more modern feel replaced ornate cocktail tables in the living room and solid cream colored rugs were added—but the look was largely created using furniture and decorative objects that were already in the house. Some areas, such as the library, were enhanced by adding designed parchment paper within the ceiling coffers.

The living room was transformed by introducing solids instead of prints and toning down the overall palette. Simple curtains were installed where heavy draperies had hung. Originally we had English embroidered draperies, typical of an English country houses, and today we have crisp, unadorned linen curtains with no swags in sight.

The master bedroom, which had evoked charming British country inn with tester bed and golden scenic fabric, was redone for a teenage daughter, and we created a large master suite down the hall. We introduced pale tones, but much of the furniture was recycled. We removed the canopy of the bed and added crisp linens. The draperies are now cream textured fabric. But thegoal was not to redecorate in the modern style. Instead we wanted to blend the couple's antiques and collections into their new lifestyle and the new millennium.

The kitchen changed only slightly. While the kitchen is the clichéd heart of the home, in this case it is completely true. After years of seeing refrigerators stocked with only Perrier or only spa food, it is refreshing to see a cooking kitchen filled with family warmth, tempting odors and yummy casseroles. It is a backdrop that contains a world into itself, and I do wonder if this family needs any other rooms at all.

Opposite and below: Classic Tudor features include a handsome slate roof, half timbering, an ornamented stone door surround at the entrance, and casement windows.

Left: Installing end-grain wood wallpaper gives the sense of a wood-paneled, clubby room without the expense or effort.

Below and opposite: The living room is now fresh and clean and the remaining traditional accessories look at home in the less cluttered setting. Simple window treatment and new contemporary rugs lightened the once-heavy look.

Below: The breakfast nook has a provincial feel, perfect for serious country cooking.

Opposite: The butler's pantry also serves as a bar and as a display area for glass and porcelain. The bold stenciling is another classic element of Americana.

Opposite: Simple lines and a pale color scheme create a welcoming bedroom. The French bench was recovered to give it a second life.

Below: This organized and soothing dressing area was originally an upstairs den.

AUDACIOUS PARIS

Above: The wealth of architectural details makes Paris a wonderful place to work.

Opposite: Tall Parisian windows are framed by elegant satin curtains and a cut velvet window seat.

Just the sound of the phrase pied à terre conjures up romance. This savvy New York couple decided to fulfill their dream of being Parisian in Paris. Paris particularly suited them as "Monsieur" travelled to Europe often on business, and Paris would be a centrally located spot to serve as his base. It was priority to find a place already full of Parisian charm and requiring little construction, a place to spend a few days or a month in luxury and comfort. While the idea of a Parisian apartment conjures up a specific Old World image, there is an enormous range of size and style. There are sprawling Haussmannian manses and tiny garrets, low-ceiling beamed medieval flats and high-ceiling ateliers, each full of its own indigenous architecture and imbued with French style.

This apartment, in a small building in the first arrondissement, was full of architectural details—both original and added by owners along the way. The new Parisians wanted to create the look and feel of a *salon* of the nineteenth and early twentieth centuries, essentially a place where friends gathered and debated social, political, and cultural issues until the wee hours of the morning—replete with crystal flutes of champagne.

Before showing me the apartment for the first time, the couple announced that it was a "hoot." What could that mean? I soon found out that the decor could only be described as the stage set for *La Cage aux Folles*—black felt walls in the master bedroom, complete with natural wood sculptures from Kamasutra, naked Gibson girls adorning the doors, and purple gilt-trimmed living room furniture. But, like Pygmalion, the bones were good, in fact, excellent. Together we set out to keep the best of what was there and to redo all that was a bit too "over-the-top."

When clients approach an interior design project, they often have possessions, large or small, that they are determined to incorporate into the scheme for their new home. In this case, it was a question of keeping features of the decor that were already in place. The floral carpet in the living room, the red walls in the entrance hall, and the architectural detail throughout were "possessions" that the apartment itself brought to the equation, establishing the color scheme of the living room and the architectural frame of the decor.

Today, this is a fantasy place filled with and to be filled with the couple's treasures. The living room boasts a camel velvet embroidered sofa, a tufted round-a-bout, velvet walls, and embroidered taffeta draperies, but all was based around the existing red, camel, and black floral carpeting. Stripping the mantel, which had been painted over in black, revealed a lovely taupe marble, handsome rather than gaudy. Everything is embellished with layers of trim, passementerie, and bespoke finishing. Inspiration came from eighteenth- and nineteenth-century chateaux. Furniture was purchased at the Marché aux Puces, and if we couldn't find it, we made it. Some of the pieces, such as the dining table, were crafted in an ebony wood by the contemporary cabinetmaker Philippe Hurel. In the master bedroom, we took an eclectic approach, ignoring the dictates of what came before. "Madame" selected lavender and taupe, her favorite colors, and we created a lovely master bedroom with velvets and taffetas from the likes of Nobilis. These were set off by mirrored crown moldings and an ingenious mirror that flips up to reveal the television.

Creating a decor in Paris is exhilarating. There is so much to choose from, from every period of history, and one of the best things about working in Paris is that the answer is always yes. The process was both fun and rewarding. The only stress was the schedule. We began September 1 with the move-in on February 2. I will admit that workmen were walking down the stairs as the owners were coming up the elevator, but essentially, together, we created *la vie en rose*.

Right: The makeup table/dressing area is concealed in a niche behind one of the padded screens. The pouf is velvet and studded with passementerie.

Below and opposite: Mirrors in the crown molding and mirrored nightstands add another level of whimsy and sparkle to the bedroom. The bed skirt is heavily embedded with passementerie that extends the purple palette of the room.

Left: A sumptuous banquette also provides storage. The Philippe Hurel dining table serves as a backdrop for many different tablescapes drawn from the owners' collection of porcelain and crystal. Wall fabric was brought to Paris from Bevilacqua in Venice.

Below: The front door is flanked by traditional portières.

Below and opposite: Living room walls are upholstered in a camel velvet fabric. The fireplace was stripped of black paint to reveal a richly grained tauple marble. The sofa is upholstered in camel mohair velvet.

Above and opposite: The entrance hall has several niches, one of which creates a sleeping nook and another a study.

Above: The reds and yellows in the stained glass window
inspired the palette of the living room.

FAMILY CLASSIC

Above: A 1950s Sputnik chandelier made of Murano glass hangs in the dining room.

Opposite: An alabaster vase is silhouetted in a niche in the living room.

The most confounding aspect of living in a big city is making a big family comfortable in an urban apartment. Space is at premium, not only for the details like closets and bathrooms, but also for the most important area of all: bedrooms.

This young family came to me with a dilemma: they loved their sprawling apartment, and they had three children installed in two bedrooms. Now they were expecting a fourth and did not know what to do. Although space planning is my specialty, and I tend to see space differently and more geometrically than many, this would be a challenge. The two existing bedrooms were large with gracious proportions, so we set to turning them into three, separate rooms for two of the children and one large "double." Fortunately, the original architecture, including the size and placement of the windows, helped achieve the goal.

The next challenge was creating a "grownup" environment for day-to-day life and adult entertaining. Although four young children in a city apartment sounds daunting, the couple did not want to compromise, and they wanted an elegant place for today and for their future. There were concessions, to be sure, such as beige sofas instead of white and more perisable fabrics, but they achieved their goal by carefully selecting the different components of the design, balancing formality and practicality. The extended family is large, and entertaining the family, much more often than on major holidays, was also an element guiding the design. The living room was designed using every inch of space. We installed banquettes on either side of the main fireplace, adding additional seating. In the dining room we recentered the room, enabling the placement of a very large dining table that accommodates sixteen.

Sometimes the challenge is to resolve the conflict between traditional architecture and modern furnishings. Here the goal was to combine luxurious furnishings with a family with four very

Right: Flanking an Art Deco console are a pair of benches by J. Robert Scott in textured silver leather.

Opposite: The playroom shows off the fantastic newspaper wall covering by Lori Weitzner and a faux shagreen table with colorful ottomans designed by Dessins.

young children, i.e., practicality. This was accomplished by using very sophisticated elements like Art Deco–inspired alabaster chandeliers, sparkling midcentury Sputnik crystal chandeliers, mother-of-pearl wall insets, high-gloss paint, and mixing them with more practical design elements such as sturdy, darker toned fabrics and patterned carpets. In the family room, we used a base color of medium gray for the walls, combining paint and grasscloth, and using a durable corduroy on the sofa, accenting it with bright colors for a happy, fun atmosphere.

In the dining room a custom-made table dominates the room, surrounded by pearlized papers on the walls. It is set off by a glamorous midcentury French chandelier.

Left: Pilasters were added to the dining room to recenter the space. The scale of the chandelier makes it an imposing element.

Opposite: Royal Copenhagen china mixes with Christofle chargers and flatware to create a regal table setting.

Left: A vintage curved sofa and a round glass and brass table mitigate the rectangularity of the living room. A series of sconces gives a soft light that reflects off the highly polished plaster walls.

Opposite: The master bedroom is filled with sensual features such as the rock crystal lamps, the reflective metal Sputnik chandelier and mirrored chests. Plum accents enliven the silvery palette.

Below: A glamorous chaise, covered in velvet, is placed in front of satin curtains, and the result is "luxe, calme, et volupté."

HISTORIC MANOR HOUSE

Above: The ottoman in the entrance gallery is upholstered in tufted cut velvet, a gesture to bygone days.

Opposite: The traditional elements of the library—fireplace and wood paneling—are enhanced by the rich jewel-toned color scheme and period furniture.

Historic houses are a category unto themselves. They come with a patina and a thousand stories. Multiple families may have lived in them—owners who updated them, first bringing them into or through the centuries and then making them comfortable to that generation's standards. Different owners take different approaches to this task. Some are simply living today's life in an old house. Others are more concerned with the integrity of the house itself. They want to update, design, and decorate to their taste, but they don't want the house, with a personality all its own, to be "upset." Historic houses do have personality: they have a DNA, they come with their bones, their atmosphere, their charisma.

Milstream Manor is no exception. The exception is the exacting clients who want to keep the integrity of the house intact and are willing to pour herculean efforts into that task. The red brick house, built in 1917, sits on a graceful property, on a gentle hill, imposing, and looking down on visitors as they approach. There is a lovely stream and a ravine that surrounds it, and outbuildings scattered here and there.

What was interesting about this project was the way the clients' taste mixed with the bones of the home. They wanted to complement the home itself, but they had no interest in stuffy, conservative traditional Americana. Their idea was more sophisticated, less cold, as American traditional tends to be, with an eye on the feeling the home would express.

During the brainstorming stage, the clients showed me pictures, but not shots of rooms cuclipped from magazines; these were actual pictures and even a record cover. From there we were able to create the smoky, jewel-toned palette, the combination of unusual textures and shapes. In fact, that was the mission, the search for the *insolite,* the hard-to-find object, the intrinsically beautiful.

Above: Millstream Manor, built in 1917 for the playwright Winchell Smith, sits on a hill above the brook.

Opposite: The regal staircase needed no embellishment.

The challenge was the merging of the architecture with the bohemian, old world look the clients desired. This was accomplished with color and texture. The architecture guided the palette with natural textures in both wood and stone, seen in the library and entrance, in the painted moldings, and even the painted plaster walls in the living room and sunroom. The furniture plans were also a challenge. The over-scaled mantel in the library as well as the openings for doors and windows left little floor space for furniture. The sunroom needed to be oriented towards the outdoors, bringing the outdoors in. The living room presented less of a problem, as its large scale allowed us to play with unusual shapes of vintage furnishings. Almost every piece was antique or vintage, and we shopped only in those markets. Newly made furniture and lighting was verboten. Many of the unusual pieces were selected with the clients at the Marché aux Puces in Paris and shipped to the house. The clients firmly appreciated the beauty, craftsmanship, and uniqueness of old things. They loved knowing that what you see is what you actually get, that each piece has a history of its own. These little bits of history add even more to the patina of the house. Every item was so carefully selected and thought about, it was a pleasure to share the wife's enthusiasm and all the personal taste she added to the design process. This was a case of the clients becoming true collaborators and bringing their own "DNA" to the equation.

Left: The grand entrance gallery boasts an antique Steinway piano as well as a period art nouveau cabinet. The custom rug was designed by Dessins for Stark Carpet. Ceiling lights are Delisle from Paris.

Opposite and below: The living room reflects the clients' taste for color and glamor, seen in the smoky palette and gold detailing at the cornice, as well as the profusion of objects assembled over the years.

Opposite: The custom dining table by Mark Luedeman boasts an ingenious rising center plateau for holiday centerpieces.

Below: The wall painting in the sunroom was commissioned by an earlier owner. The coffee table is a replica of an antique French game table, painted in the colors of the room.

Opposite: In the kitchen, crisp, white cabinetry is a foil for the colorful bistro chairs, majolica, and earthy wall coverings.

Below: The sofa in the family room is oriented to the tall windows in the bay. The classic Penny ottoman works for serving while taking in the view.

BEVERLY HILLS
MEDITERRANEAN

Above: The shape of the lanterns complements the curved ceilings.

Opposite: The setting is compelling, with inside and outside in harmony.

At the end of *Casablanca* Humphrey Bogart tells Claude Rains, "I think this is the beginning of a beautiful friendship." Who knew in 1997 I would have a lifelong friendship with the young bachelor who hired me to design his first apartment in the San Remo in New York City? Some fourteen years later, he called from Los Angeles to ask me to create the interiors of his new Beverly Hills house, designed by architect Richard Landry.

In some ways, this home was more of a challenge than our first project together, since the architecture, the setting, and the art and family heirlooms acquired over the years all had to be combined into a cohesive ensemble. The house itself has the look and feeling of a Tuscan villa, with varying levels and planes that give the sense of an old building that had been added onto over time. The overall effect is traditional, regal, warm, and inviting. There is a lovely rhythm from interior to exterior, with almost every room opening onto beautifully planted terraces. The house is oriented to ensure privacy, and once inside the gates, there is a feeling of a secluded oasis.

Shallow arches and beams enhance the interior architecture. The principal feature is a double-height space beneath a vaulted brick ceiling. A massive stone wall pierced by arched openings at both levels defines the space as entrance hall and living room. An elegant loggia connects the second floor spaces horizontally. The materials—stone and brick walls and ceilings, enormous limestone fireplaces, and robust woodwork—combine to create a home filled with atmosphere that is shaped by the interior design.

Like all projects, this home starts with the client, who is traditional through and through. Since our first project together, he has always been more comfortable with traditional design and furnishings. From our earlier shopping days at the Marché aux Puces in Paris to today's excursions to La Cienega in Los Angeles, we have always been on the prowl for traditional, warm, rich, and unusual pieces, what the French would call *insolite*.

In spite of, or perhaps because of, the finishes, color plays an important role in the decor, as the textures of so many natural materials give the home its own palette. Earth tones and neutrals are subdued so that the furnishings and art collection can come forward. One of my client's major complaints at the outset was that the rooms looked too dull, too bland. The colors we added range from cinnamon and corals to chocolate, browns and creams which subtly combine to create a serene envelope for a collection of European paintings.

Opposite: The main entrance gallery is dramatically enhanced by handsome stonework.

Below: The living room incorporates a large circular bar as well as an important fireplace wall.

Opposite: Windows in the living room are arranged in two bands, with generous wall space between to hang paintings from the clients' collection.

Below: In contrast to the openness of the living room, the library feels intimate and enclosed.

Left: Arched openings punctuate the walls, creating views through the interior space.

Opposite: Maison Gatti bistro chairs and Italian ceramic add color to the kitchen.

Below: The glass-fronted wine cellar is adjacent to the dining room.

Below: The breakfast room is covered with mixed Venetian fabrics and patterns, some from Fortuny.

Opposite: A guest room opens onto a private terrace.

Left and below: A serene oval pool and Tuscan-style pool house are nestled into the landscape.

Fireman pulling drunk out of a burning bed: You darned, fool, that'll teach you to smoke in bed. *Drunk:* I wasn't smoking in bed, it was on fire when I laid down.

COSMOPOLITAN COOL

Above: Custom hardware from Guerin exemplifies craftsmanship.

Opposite: The curved base of the Art Deco console inspired the marble pattern on the foyer floor.

In the 1920s Rosario Candela emerged as the master of the Park Avenue apartment building, creating apartments to replicate the lifestyle of Gilded Age mansions as the wealthy transitioned to vertical living. Candela designs are set apart from the majority of Upper East Side buildings by the graciousness and elegance of their floor plans, the proportions of the rooms, and the character of the architectural details.

This apartment represents the taste and refinement of its owners overlaid on the delicateness of the Candela standard. Here a combination of classic taste with a young, fresh twist invigorates the generously proportioned rooms, illustrating that everything old is new again.

There is a juxtaposition of traditional finishes, including marble and reclaimed European wooden flooring, with modern art and midcentury antiques. These materials such as marble and parquet would have been at home in an original apartment of this genre, but when coupled with twentieth-century furnishings, a different look and feeling emerges.

Over the past eighty years, successive owners made many changes to the apartment, but not all enhanced the original. Ferguson and Shamamian Architects set that right. To restore the apartment to its former glory in a comtemporary context, the moldings and architectural features were completely revamped. The apartment was stripped down to its bare bones and rebuilt in a new incarnation of the original layout. Ceiling designs, moldings, and wall treatments are all newly designed. These are classic in inspiration and contemporary in the way they are used, enhancing the structural grace of the apartment and seamlessly integrated into it. In every case, these moldings and ceiling designs mediate between the contemporary furniture and the classic frame of the architecture.

Opposite: The library was completely rebuilt. Dessins designed the ceiling molding and decor; Ferguson and Shamamian Architects produced the handsome woodwork inlaid with bronze.

Above left: A bar is concealed behind paneling to the left of the fireplace.

Above right: An enfilade extends from the front hall through the living room to the library.

Color is another element that ties the traditional architecture of the apartment to its more modern interior. In many contemporary settings, white is the predominant background color. But in this case, against this neutral base, rich colors such as cobalt blue in the living room and dining room and Chinese red in the library are used as accents to enliven the rooms. This strategy also works for the future since the accents can be easily changed to re-invent the look. The richness of the hard finishes, such as stone floors, the rich gray and sanguine in the entrance gallery and the paneling, such as the library's chestnut hue, showcases how color tone enhances the Art Deco period pieces as well as the contemporary art collection.

The architectural process did take a bit of time because of the complexities and intricacies of the design and the building's summer work rules; the clients, however, were unflappable. They were involved and enthusiastic and took all stumbling blocks in stride. I have boundless respect for these clients and this is among my favorite projects since the clients were savvy enough to enjoy the best parts of the design process and ignore the rest.

The clients wanted their home to be fun, a happy place where they could raise a young family but they also wanted an elegant and chic atmosphere. This is an excellent example of a fluid marriage of architecture and decoration, and the apartment now exactly represents who the clients are and what they wished for their family life.

Left: In the living room, original details, including the cornice and marble fireplace, are juxtaposed with a glamorous gold-leaf ceiling.

Below: The Yves Klein coffee table anchors the color scheme.

Opposite and below: Dessins designed moldings for the dining room ceiling and walls to create visual interest and suggest niches and sections in the space. The rock crystal chandelier by Mathieu Lustrerie above the table is at once functional and a work of art.

Opposite and below: Dessins created a tufted niche to showcase a period Jules Leleu buffet.

Above and right: Two baths extend the rich materials of the apartment: mother-of-pearl walls, a carved stone sink, and a crystal basin and pedestal.

Opposite: A blue stone backsplash and red Hermès dishes and Knoll chairs add color and interest to the kitchen. The ceiling lights are by Jean Perzel.

Opposite: In the master bedroom, the shallow bed niche adds definition to a flat wall and showcases this sumptuous bed. Nightstands are by Lorin Marsh.

Below left: Shallow cabinets were added between the windows to house necessities such as the TV. Églomisé panels by Miriam Ellner are a luxurious touch.

Below right: A soft blue and gray palette creates a serene atmosphere in the study.

Below and opposite: The dressing room has distinct areas created for different functions. Closet doors are enhanced with a crisscross motif over mirrors and hardware in nickel and brass by Guerin. Each bathroom has a unique vanity designed by Dessins for this apartment.

Left: A vintage lucite swinging chair adds a fun element to this room.

Below: A custom vanity and patent-leather walls create a "cool" guest bathroom.

Below and opposite: A triple niche makes this little girl's room feel both both cozy and organizied. The custom lampshade chandelier is trimmed with a pink crystal ball by Denis Collura.

PALM BEACH ELEGANCE

Above: The coffered ceiling in the library is painted in a classical motif.

Opposite: The loggia overlooking the pool is a serene dining space.

It is too easy to give a client a "Palm Beach look" or a "penthouse look" or a "country inn look" and so on. The "look" is often associated with a certain locale, but all clients bring their own desires and fantasies to their project. My mission is to make my clients' homes individual and personal, as individual as they are.

This Spanish-influenced house has many of the trappings of the architecture and design of Palm Beach. Giving onto a waterway, the house is relatively new construction, designed with an eye on the Palm Beach of yesteryear. Stucco, columns, stone floors: these were the givens. The clients had worked with me on several projects in New York and on Long Island so I was acquainted with their taste. They like traditional but not stuffy, they like whimsy and interesting objects and accessories, but most of all they have always been receptive to new and interesting ideas. In retrospect, they have always been pleased with the risks we have taken. Compared to other projects we have created together, there was not too much opportunity for architectural change in this house. We moved a doorway and a column to make the flow between rooms fluid, but the bones were set and we had to do the dressing.

While it was important that the rooms worked together, each had its own architectural bent and its own flavor. The living room had to be white with its stately columns and water views; anything else would have fought the exterior. To take advantage of the space, it was designed with a back-to-back sofa, one sofa facing the view and the other facing the music area. Upholstered in white, they were embellished with tapestry borders embroidered down the center of each cushion. The walls were left primarily blank for artworks, but tall bibliothèques balanced the columns while still leaving a space for art. The library is trimmed in oak, with deep wooden coffers in the ceiling. I added a traditional period limestone mantel to create a focal point, an architectural element that balanced some of the heavy woodwork. Rather than fight this heaviness, I enhanced it by adding sumptuous embossed leather walls, similar to those found

in eighteenth-century French chateaux. A large oak bibliothèque and painted coffers continue the detailing of the room surround.

The dining room was bare by comparison. A white rectangle with no architectural features and no view, the room seemed sad. Starting with framed tapestry panels found in Paris, I created a fantasy room that would be the backdrop for lavish dinner parties. To add architectural interest, I angled the corners, but not with the expected straight angles. I used curves, creating two half moon china cabinets with buffet centers that could be used for storage and serving, and complemented them on the other side of the room by mirroring them with curved doors. All were hand-painted with tiny flowers to match the period frames on the tapestries.

The master bedroom was also uninteresting. Here I clad the walls with limestone bricks, floor to ceiling, installed a vintage limestone mantel, and wherever there was an empty spot that could not be tiled, I had hand painted limestone applied.

Traditional in feeling, yes, but every area has a twist. In this project the inspiration was taken as it came, sometimes architectural as in the dining room, sometimes from the very unusual objects we found.

Opposite: The gray of the traditional French painted cabinets becomes an accent in the all-white palette.

Below: The house is designed in the Mediterranean style so typical of Palm Beach.

Opposite and below: Carved stone column capitals and intricate ironwork make the space feel elegant and traditional. Antiques and artwork drawn from European and Asian sources include a Chagall lithograph, a Chinese console with an English mirror above, and Moroccan-style banquettes.

Opposite and below: The living room sofas were embellished with tapestry panels to enhance the bespoke feeling. Chairs were copied from an eighteenth-century French salon, trimmed generously with passementerie.

Opposite and below: The walls of the library were clad with tooled leather, often found in Loire Valley chateaux in France. Carved stone column capitals support a glass-topped table.

Left: The dining room is a fantasy that began with the framed tapestry panels. The cabinets and matching carved doors were painted with the same floral motif and filled with a collection of antique china.

Right: The walls of the master bedroom are entirely clad in stone to create an unexpected texture, while the moldings are painted trompe l'oeil limestone.

Below: A Recamier completes the antique French look.

SOURCES

Bernd Goeckler
Antiques
30 East 10th Street
New York

Carlos de la Puente
209 East 59th Street
New York

Silver Peacock
979 Third Avenue
New York

Holland & Sherry
979 Third Avenue
New York

John Salibello
229 East 60th Street
New York

Lee Caliccio
306 East 61st Street
New York

John Rosselli
306 East 61st Street
New York

Mantiques Modern
146 West 22nd Street
New York

L'Art de Vivre
978 Lexington Avenue
New York

Sentimento
306 East 61st Street
New York

Frette
799 Madison Avenue
New York

Eric Appel
306 East 61st Street
New York

Craig Van den Brulle
192 Elizabeth Street
New York

Argosy Bookstore
116 East 59th Street
New York

Bernardaud
499 Park Avenue
New York

Maison Gerard
53 East 10th Street
New York

Venfield
227 East 60th Street
New York

William Wayne
850 Lexington Avenue
New York

High Style Deco
224 West 18th Street
New York

Casa di Bianco
866 Lexington Avenue
New York

1st Dibs
200 Lexington Avenue
New York

Flair
88 Grand Street
New York

Jean de Merry
979 Third Avenue
New York

Mecox
257 Country Road 39A
Southampton, New York

English Country
Antiques
26 Snake Hollow Road
Bridgehampton
New York

The General
Home Store
100 Park Place
East Hampton
New York

Barney's
660 Madison Avenue
New York

Le Douze
12 Rue Jacob
Paris

Espaces 54
54 Rue Mazarine
Paris

Galerie l' Arc
en Seine
31 Rue de Seine
Paris

Galerie Jean-Louis
Danant
36 Avenue Matignon
Paris

Galerie Makassar-
France
19 Avenue Matignon
Paris

Galerie André Hayat
23 Rue de Lille
Paris

Galerie Sylvain
Levy-Alban
14 Rue de Beaune
Paris

Hermès
17 Rue de Seine
Paris

Galeries des Lampes
9 Rue de Beaune
Paris

Delisle
4 Rue Parc Royal
Paris

Jean Perzel
3 Rue de la Cité
Universitaire
Paris

Andrea Arreghe
Traslucido
Via Maggio 11r
Florence

Flair
Lungarno Corsini 24r
Florence

CREDITS

Palm Beach Pied à Terre
Nick Sargent

Country Calm
Francis Hammond

City Chic
Durston Saylor and Francis Hammond

Palm Desert Dreaming
Grey Crawford

American Country
Matt Wargo

Park Avenue Modern
Francis Hammond

Suburban Savvy
Francis Hammond

Audacious Paris
Francis Hammond

Family Classic
Francis Hammond

Historic Manor House
Matt Wargo

Beverly Hills Mediterranean
Gray Crawford

Cosmopolitan Cool
Francis Hammond

Palm Beach Elegance
Kim Sargent